A Day in the Life: Rain Forest Animals

Howler Monkey

Anita Ganeri

Heinemann Library
Chicago, IL

www.heinemannraintree.com
Visit our website to find out
more information about
Heinemann-Raintree books.

To order:

☎ Phone 888-454-2279

🖳 Visit www.heinemannraintree.com
to browse our catalog and order online.

Edited by Nancy Dickmann, Rebecca Rissman, and
Catherine Veitch
Designed by Steve Mead
Picture research by Mica Brancic
Originated by Capstone Global Library
Printed and bound in China by South China Printing Com-
pany Ltd

14 13 12 11 10
10 9 8 7 6 5 4 3 2

**Library of Congress Cataloging-in-
Publication Data**
Ganeri, Anita
  Howler monkey / Anita Ganeri.—1st ed.
    p. cm.—(A day in the life. Rain forest animals)
  Includes bibliographical references and index.
  ISBN 978-1-4329-4113-0 (hc)—ISBN 978-1-4329-4124-6
(pb) 1. Howler monkeys—Juvenile literature. I. Title.
  QL737.P915G36 2011
  599.8'55—dc22   2010001137

Acknowledgments
We would like to thank the following for permission to
reproduce photographs: Alamy pp. 16 (© Jonathan Hewitt),
20 (© Arco Images GmbH/Therin-Weise), 23 energy (© M.
Krofel Wildlife), 23 troop (© Jonathan Hewitt), 13 (© M.
Krofel Wildlife); Corbis pp. 4 (Terra/© Theo Allofs), 23
mammal (Terra/© Theo Allofs); FLPA pp. 10 (Minden
Pictures), 11 (Minden Pictures/© Pete Oxford), 18 (© Jurgen
& Christine Sohns), 21 (© Martin B Withers), 22 (Minden
Pictures/Kevin Schafer); Getty Images pp. 19 (National
Geographic/Joel Sartore), 23 ticks (National Geographic/Joel
Sartore); Photolibrary pp. 5 (Picture Press/J & C Sohns), 7
(Juniors Bildarchiv), 9 (Picture Press/J & C Sohns), 12 (Juniors
Bildarchiv), 14 (Animals Animals/Peter Weimann), 15 (age
footstock), 17 (Imagestate RM/Jeffrey Rich), 6 (age fotostock/
Enrique R Aguirre); Shutterstock p. 23 rain forest (© Szefei).

Cover photograph of a black howler monkey reproduced with
permission of Photolibrary (Juniors Bildarchiv).

Back cover photographs of (left) a howler baby reproduced
with permission of Corbis (Terra/© Theo Allofs) and (right)
howler tail reproduced with permission of Photolibrary (Juniors Bildarchiv).

We would like to thank Michael Bright for his invaluable help
in the preparation of this book.

Every effort has been made to contact copyright holders
of material reproduced in this book. Any omissions will
be rectified in subsequent printings if notice is given to
the publishers.

All the internet addresses (URLs) given in this book were valid
at the time of going to press. However, due to the dynamic
nature of the Internet, some addresses may have changed
or ceased to exist since publication. While the author and
publishers regret any inconvenience this may cause readers, no
responsibility for any such changes can be accepted by either
the author or the publishers.

Contents

Some words are in bold, **like this**. You can find them in the glossary on page 23.

What Is a Howler Monkey?

A howler monkey is a **mammal**.

Many mammals have hairy bodies and feed their babies milk.

black howler

There are different types of howler monkeys.

There are black howlers, brown howlers, red howlers, and mantled howlers.

What Do Howler Monkeys Look Like?

Howler monkeys have large bodies and long tails.

Male howler monkeys are much bigger than females.

male

female

Male black howler monkeys have black fur and females have brown fur.

Baby black howler monkeys have brown fur when they are born.

Where Do Howler Monkeys Live?

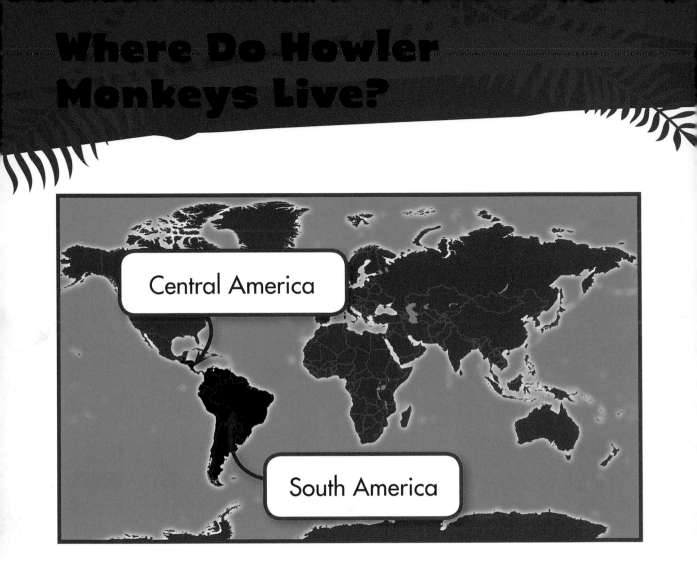

Howler monkeys live in the **rain forests** of Central America and South America.

It is warm and wet in the rain forest all year long.

Howler monkeys spend most of their time in the treetops.

They do not come down to the ground very often.

What Do Howler Monkeys Do in the Morning?

Howler monkeys wake up when the sun rises.

They sit in the trees and start howling very loudly.

The howling warns other monkeys to keep away from this patch of forest.

Afterward, the howler monkeys start looking for food.

How Do Howler Monkeys Move?

tail

During the day, howler monkeys move through the treetops to look for food.

They grip onto the branches with their hands, feet, and tail.

A howler monkey uses its long tail as an extra arm.

It has a bare patch of skin underneath its tail to help it grip the branches.

What Do Howler Monkeys Eat and Drink?

Howler monkeys mainly eat different kinds of leaves.

They also eat fruit, such as figs, and flowers.

When a howler monkey is thirsty, it dips its hand into a pool of water in a tree hole.

There is a lot of rain water in a rain forest.

Do Howler Monkeys Live in Groups?

Howler monkeys live in groups of about 20 monkeys.

A group is known as a **troop**.

baby

A baby howler monkey stays close to its mother.

During the day, it clings to its mother's fur and rides on her back.

What Do Howler Monkeys Do in the Afternoon?

In the afternoon, the troop of howler monkeys stops for a rest in the treetops.

This is because the leaves they eat do not give them very much **energy**.

The monkeys also clean each other's fur.

They use their fingers to pick off leaves, bark, and **ticks**.

What Do Howler Monkeys Do at Night?

In the evening, howler monkeys look for more leaves to eat.

Then they start howling again to let other **troops** know where they are.

The howler monkeys go to sleep in the treetops, while sitting on a branch.

They curl their tails tightly around the branch so they do not fall off.

Howler Monkey Body Map

tail

fur

eye

mouth

leg

Glossary

energy power to move or grow

mammal animal that feeds its babies milk. Most mammals have hair or fur.

rain forest thick forest with very tall trees and a lot of rain

ticks tiny creature that clings to animals and sucks their blood

troop group of monkeys

Find Out More

Books

Bredeson, Carmen. *Baby Animals of the Tropical Rain Forest.*
  Berkeley Heights, NJ: Enslow Elementary, 2009.
Donovan, Sandra. *Howler Monkeys.* Chicago:
  Raintree, 2003.

Websites

http://animals.nationalgeographic.com/animals/mammals/
  howler-monkey/
www.a-z-animals.com/animals/howler-monkey/

Index